There is a fax machine in the school office. The fax machine is used to send and receive copies of printed pages through the telephone line. It is much quicker than sending the pages in the mail.

There are computers in the classroom. The computers are used to play learning games. Everyone in the classroom uses the computers.

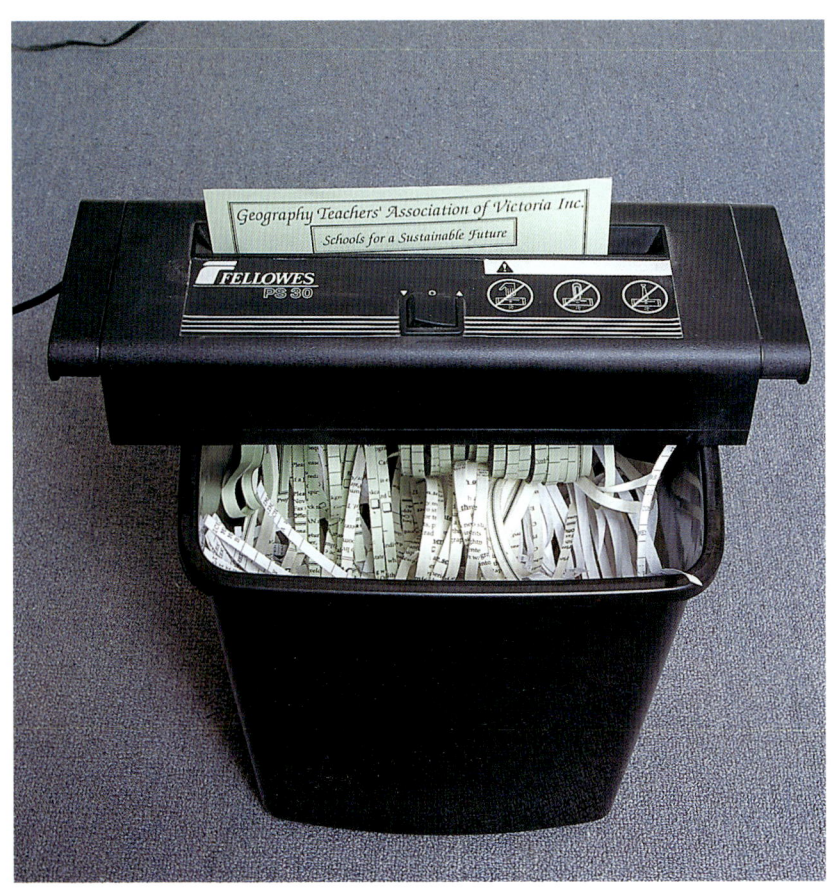

There is a paper shredder in the school office. The paper shredder cuts up paper into small strips. The shredded paper is recycled.

There is a television and a VCR in the school library. The television is used to show science, health, and language programs.
The VCR is used to show videotapes.

There is an answering machine in the school office. It is used to record messages when there is no one to answer the telephone. It is turned off when people are in the office.

There are calculators in the classroom. The calculators are used to work out math problems. They do not make mistakes — unless the people using them do!

Machines in the School

Focus: Materials
Information
Systems

PETER SLOAN &
SHERYL SLOAN

There is a photocopier in the school library. The photocopier is used to make copies of worksheets, letters, and books. It saves a lot of time because it copies pages quickly.